Vet cadets

Written by Richard Johnson

Illustrated by Martin Chatterton

Collins

The town of Veryboring, northern Iceland, 10:00 p.m.

Once a year, Grandma Jona takes her bath. That's her there, walking to the hot pools. Iceland is full of lovely hot pools, geysers and steamy stuff like that.

I'M OFF TO TAKE MY BATH!

Everyone wished Grandma Jona all the best. Floki the fishmonger, who was fermenting shark, gave her a wave.

She's off to take her bath!

I'M OFF TO TAKE MY BATH!

Katla looked up from the coffee she was brewing and gave a wink.

Grandma got ready to dive into her bubbly, steaming, totally toasty hot bath.

But Grandma Jona bounced off the hot pool!

The hot pools weren't hot at all. They were frozen solid! It was the first time ever that Grandma Jona couldn't take her bath. Something was very wrong indeed.

Meanwhile, while her Mum and Dad were downstairs frying kleinur, Viktoria Vilmarsdottir was fast asleep.

If you dream about white sheep in Iceland it may mean it's going to snow.

Also asleep were her special pets: Rex the dog, Bloo the cat, Nomi a puffin who slept standing and Bob, a fish Viktoria had rescued.

4

Viktoria's pets weren't the only ones who were special though; on certain nights, when the calls came in, Viktoria Vilmarsdottir transformed into Vet Girl ...

... ready to treat any mythical creature who needed help!

Suddenly, an alert came in at the Command Centre (aka Bob's Bowl) ...

We've got incoming, people! CODE RED. The hot pools are frozen over. Looks like a job for THE VET CADETS!

Bob, get it up on the big screen!

5

7

In no time at all the team changed into their Vet Cadet outfits.

VET GIRL
Team Leader

BLOO
Vambulance Pilot

BOB
Command Centre

REX
X-Ray Spex

NOMI
Nurse

The hidden person was right about the entrance to the glacier. Vet Girl knocked on the small wooden door.

In Iceland, it's lucky to say these numbers when you knock on wood.

There was a loud creak as the small wooden door slid open. The entrance to the glacier was dark and spooky. None of them really wanted to go inside. But they had received the distress signal and the Vet Cadets never, ever let anyone down. Swallowing hard, and with Viktoria's head torch lighting the way, they took a few nervous steps into the dark glacier.

Follow me. I hope this lava tunnel hasn't got any hot lava left!

I can't stand lava!

There was someone or something at the end of the tunnel.

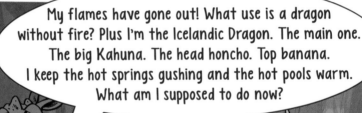

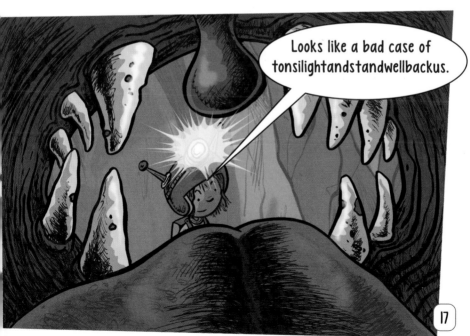

Viktoria's special Vet Guide

Now, let me see ...

No, that's not right.

Have you ever seen a whale sneeze? It's disgusting. Their nose is on top of their head!

Ewww!

No, that's not what we're looking for either.

Did you know that trolls turn to stone if they are outside after sunrise?

Um, cool fact, Rex.

Aha! Here we are!

Spicy Smoothie
To get your dragon firing again.

Ingredients:
The spiciest of black pepper.
The hottest of hot mustard.
One really, really hot chilli.

Bob! Come in, Bob! Locate black pepper! Everyone back to the Vambulance!

The Vet Team followed the peppercorns towards a deserted warehouse. Nomi picked up the peppercorns as they went along.

OK. I'll pick them up then!

Keep going, Rex! A warehouse!

The Extra Strong Super Pepper is inside!

There's no way we'll get past that fence!

So now can we go home? I need to get rid of all these peppercorns I've been picking up.

Nomi! You're a genius. The peppercorns! Of course! We've already got enough for the dragon's cure.

Bob. Pepper secured. Where's the next ingredient?

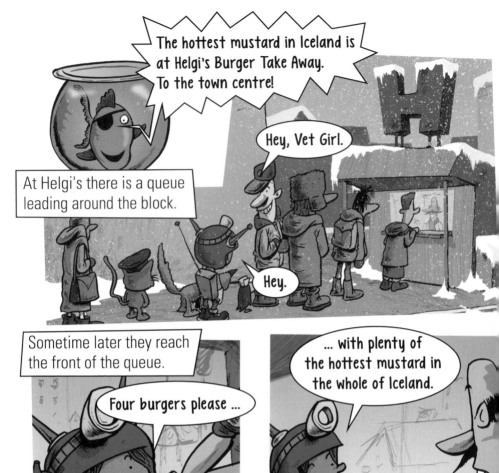

The hottest mustard in Iceland is at Helgi's Burger Take Away. To the town centre!

Hey, Vet Girl.

At Helgi's there is a queue leading around the block.

Hey.

Sometime later they reach the front of the queue.

Four burgers please ...

... with plenty of the hottest mustard in the whole of Iceland.

Sorry Vet Girl, no mustard tonight.

It's my grandfather's special recipe. He's gone on holiday and locked the mustard in the safe without telling us the combination.

Oh no. Have you tried to guess it?

22

Of course we have but with no success. You're welcome to try. But if you can guess it correctly you must be the luckiest girl in Iceland.

The door slid open revealing pots of Grandpa Helgi's super-hot hot mustard.

23

Inside Farmer Freyja's greenhouse were thousands of chillies. But where was the purple one?

Here, chilli, chilli, chilli.

Red chilli. Green chilli. Red chilli. Green chilli.

I can't stand chillies.

There are too many chillies. We'll never find the purple one. Not in a million years. Hold on ...

Found it!

Back to the dragon's cave!

The Vet Cadets raced back to the dragon's cave.

We've got all we need to make this smoothie!

Inside the cave they began to blend the ingredients.

Black pepper first! AH-CHOO!

Add a nice dollop of mustard!

And one SUPER-HOT CHILLI!

Vet Girl poured the potion into a beaker.

HOLD ON TIGHT, I'M GOING TO BLEND!

Time to see if this smoothie works.

The cure for the dragon's sore throat worked!
In no time at all, the hot pools were hot again.
The Vet Cadets scrambled into the Vambulance
and whooshed off back to the Vet Cave.

PROBLEM-SOLVING WITH THE VET CADETS

PROBLEM: NO HOT WATER

SOLUTION: GET THE VET CADETS!

VET GIRL
Team Leader

PROBLEM: A GRUMPY DRAGON WITH NO FLAMES

SOLUTION: FIND A COLD REMEDY

Spicy Smoothie
To get your dragon firing again.

Ingredients:
The spiciest of black pepper.
The hottest of hot mustard.
One really, really hot chilli.

PROBLEM: THE PEPPER BOAT HAS SAILED AWAY

SOLUTION: FIND SPILLED PEPPER